Intentional Joy

Discover Strategies to Create Joy for Yourself and Others

Study Guide

Jacquelyn Lynn

Publisher: Tuscawilla Creative Services, LLC
Cover Design and Interior Art: Jerry D. Clement
Production and Composition: Tuscawilla Creative Services

Tuscawilla Creative Services, LLC
P. O. Box 1501
Goldenrod, FL 32733-1501

www.CreateTeachInspire.com

For bulk purchase information, including customization options, email info@contactTCS.com

Intentional Joy: Discover Strategies to Create Joy for Yourself and Others (Study Guide) / Jacquelyn Lynn – 1st ed.

ISBN 978-1-941826-25-6

Contents

Welcome

Intentional Joy is a guide designed to help you make the most of your study of *Finding Joy in the Morning: You* can *make it through the night.* If you don't already have a copy of that book, ordering details are in the back of this book.

This study guide can be used alone or in a group. You have plenty of room for notes, but how much you share with others is your decision.

If you are using this study guide in a group, remember that no one is there to solve problems or provide all the answers. No one needs to be a Biblical scholar. If you choose to designate a group leader, that person's primary role should be that of a facilitator. Your collective goal is to stay organized, consistent, and confident as you work through this study. You'll grow in your own faith as you help others do the same.

It's important to be sensitive to the issues and problems of the members of your group. If someone is struggling with something major, take the time necessary to care for that person. If possible and appropriate, do it within the group. If not, encourage the person to seek help from another qualified source, such as a pastor, Stephen Minister, or even an appropriate licensed healthcare provider.

If you are in a group, everyone should contribute. Invite people to share in a gentle, reassuring way. It is not necessary for every member of the group to respond to every discussion question, but it's important that everyone have the opportunity to share their thoughts and experiences.

The *Intentional Joy* study guide is based on ten sessions, but you can combine or divide sessions as necessary to accommodate your schedule and the needs of your members.

Each session reviews the discussion questions in *Finding Joy in the Morning* and includes some additional questions and exercises. You may choose to go through all of the questions and exercises or select only some of

them to discuss; make that decision based on the structure and dynamics of your particular group.

A specially-designed notes page is at the end of each section. Use the left column to record your notes of what others have said. Use the right column to write down your thoughts and ideas.

Ground Rules for a Group Study

Ground rules help create a warm, welcoming atmosphere and set clear expectations for the group and the study. Go over the ground rules in detail during the first session, then quickly review them at the beginning of each subsequent session. Be sure everyone in the group is clear on these recommended basic ground rules:

- **Confidentiality.** What is said in the group stays in the group. Everyone must be comfortable that what they share about themselves will not be revealed outside the group.

- **Participation.** Everyone should have the opportunity to contribute to the discussion.

- **Listen.** When one person is speaking, everyone else should be listening actively. No interrupting, no talking over someone else, no telling others what they should do.

- **No judgments.** Don't judge others or yourself. Leave the judging to God.

- **Tone.** Keep it positive. You want people to be honest and open, but avoid letting the discussion deteriorate into a gripe session.

- **Open and close with prayer.** Intentionally invite God into the group as you begin each session and thank him when you are finished.

You may want to establish additional guidelines for your group, such as starting and ending on time (or not—some groups will be more flexible in this area than others), whether you will have beverages and snacks, set-up and clean-up of the meeting space, and other issues related to meeting structure.

1   We're Not in this Alone

The fundamental message of *Finding Joy in the Morning* is not one of self-help but rather of I-can't-do-it-alone. Though it is human nature to want to be in complete control of the situations and circumstances we must deal with, life is not something we are made to handle alone. We need God and each other. We are made to be part of God's family, dependent on God and on others.

That dependency is a magnificent two-way street. We are not just receivers of God's grace, mercy and wisdom, we are his wonderful hands in this world—hands that are used to give and receive in beautiful interconnectivity.

If we try to do things on our own, we will not only fail in the end, we will be miserable along the way. That we are dependent on God is not a burden, it's not a crutch, it's something to be celebrated. Accepting and celebrating our dependence on God and one another is the key to knowing peace in this chaotic world.

Discussion questions (found on page 11 of *Finding Joy in the Morning*, 2nd edition):

- Who are the people in your life who support and sustain you? Think about what they mean to you. Have you shared that with them, either by telling them in person or writing to them? How did they respond?

_____

_____

_____

_____

- Have you ever been in a crisis situation and been helped by a total stranger? How did it make you feel?

_____

_____

_____

_____

_____

- Think about ways to maintain your relationship with God when you are not in crisis. How can you apply them to your life?

_____

_____

_____

_____

_____

Additional discussion questions:

- How good are you at sharing pain and suffering with a fellow believer who is hurting? How good are you at rejoicing with someone who is celebrating? Which comes easier for you? Why?

_____

_____

_____

_____

_____

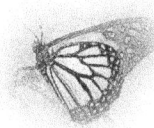

- Have you ever felt that you were part of a unit where all the parts worked together for a common goal? How was that cohesiveness developed and maintained?

_____

_____

_____

_____

_____

- How do you feel about your place in the body of Christ?

_____

_____

_____

_____

_____

Scripture

Look up the following scripture passages in the Bible translation of your choice. Write them down in the space provided. Discuss how the message can be applied to our world in general and your life in particular. Pray on these passages.

Hebrews 10:24-25

_____

_____

_____

_____

_____

_____

Romans 12:4-5

_____

_____

_____

_____

_____

_____

Acts 2:46-47

_____

_____

_____

_____

_____

_____

What can you do to add joy to your life?

_____

_____

_____

_____

_____

_____

_____

Close with prayer. Use your own prayer or the one on page 9 of _Finding Joy in the Morning_.

Notes	My thoughts

2   A Child of God

We are all children of God. We have a Heavenly Father who loves us mightily and wonderfully and who is always there.

There is nothing else in our human experience that compares to the love of a parent for a child. Creating another human being establishes a powerful bond, a love that is so deep and strong it must be experienced to be understood and believed. As awesome as that is, God's love for us is so much more because it's not restricted by our human limitations.

A key difference between our relationship with God as one of his children and our relationship with our human parents is the issue of dependency and purpose. Even though we are meant to live in community with one another, God designed us to grow up and achieve a degree of independence from our worldly parents, but we will always be dependent on our Heavenly Father.

As children of God, we are heirs of God—heirs to an inheritance that will last for eternity and is more valuable than we can imagine. Not even the biggest lottery jackpot on earth compares to what all God's children have within their reach.

Even as we take joy in what God gives, we must also recognize that we have responsibilities. God made everything and every one of us for a purpose. He wants us as his children to live out his purpose for our lives.

All of God's children are different. There is no one else in the world exactly like you, and there never will be. It's God's way of letting each of us know how special we are. We all have our own unique spiritual gifts that qualify us to carry out God's will for us.

When we accept our heritage as children of God, understand God's purpose for us and follow his will, we know true joy.

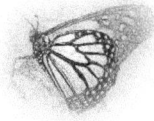

Discussion questions (found on page 33 of *Finding Joy in the Morning*, 2nd edition):

- Think about some of the labels you have carried with you throughout your life. How does adding "child of God" to that list make you feel?

  _____

  _____

  _____

  _____

- What does being a child of God mean to you?

  _____

  _____

  _____

  _____

- Do you know the purpose for which God created you? If so, what is it?

  _____

  _____

  _____

  _____

- How did you come to know God's purpose for you?

  _____

  _____

  _____

  _____

- What is preventing you from living out the purpose God has for you?

_____

_____

_____

_____

Additional discussion questions:

- Do you feel more like a child of God or a distant relative? What can you do in the coming week to improve your relationship with God and accept the fact that you are a child of God?

_____

_____

_____

_____

- What does it mean to you that you are not God's slave or property, but his child?

_____

_____

_____

_____

- The Bible is clear that we will experience troubles and challenges in this world. How has pain helped you grow?

_____

_____

_____

_____

Scripture

Look up the following scripture passages in the Bible translation of your choice. Write them down in the space provided. Discuss how the message can be applied to our world in general and your life in particular. Pray on these passages.

John 1:12

_____

_____

_____

_____

_____

_____

Deuteronomy 6:2

_____

_____

_____

_____

_____

_____

Psalm 16:11

_____

_____

_____

_____

_____

_____

What can you do to add joy to your life?

_____

_____

_____

_____

_____

_____

_____

_____

_____

_____

_____

_____

_____

_____

_____

_____

_____

_____

_____

_____

_____

_____

Close with prayer. Use your own prayer or the one on page 31 of _Finding Joy in the Morning_.

Notes	My thoughts

3   Biblical Faith

Worldly faith is defined as *complete trust or confidence in someone or something*. This type of faith is usually based on our personal experiences. Biblical faith is different. Biblical faith comes from the heart and goes far beyond what we have physical evidence for.

Faith is not religion. It's not magic. And it's not mere hope. Faith means you believe *in* God and, equally important, that you believe God. You take him at his word, all the time, in everything. And you trust him completely, not just with your eternal life but with your day-to-day earthly life.

We are made to believe in something. People who don't believe in God will believe something else. It's not that they believe *in* something evil, but they often believe the messages from that source—messages that say it's okay to commit immoral acts, to lie, to cheat, to be jealous, to engage in violence or to otherwise hurt themselves or others. That's why God wants us to have faith in him and to trust and obey his word.

In this world, faith is a work in progress. Our faith will be tested, but as we work on it intentionally, it will strengthen over time. Strong faith is not insurance against troubles and hard times. Rather, it's assurance that you will never face the troubles and hard times alone.

Discussion questions (found on page 47 of *Finding Joy in the Morning*, 2nd edition):

■   How do you define faith?

_____

_____

- How would you describe your faith in God?

_____

_____

_____

_____

- What experiences have you had that strengthened your faith in God? What was it about those experiences that made your faith stronger?

_____

_____

_____

_____

_____

- In what areas of your life do you find it most difficult to trust God?

_____

_____

_____

_____

_____

- In what areas of your life do you find it easy to trust God?

_____

_____

_____

_____

Additional discussion questions:

- What are some words that describe your present level of faith? Why did you choose those words?

  _____

  _____

  _____

  _____

- What has your faith cost you? How has it benefited you?

  _____

  _____

  _____

  _____

- What are some things that can weaken your faith?

  _____

  _____

  _____

  _____

- How do you guard against the things that can weaken your faith?

  _____

  _____

  _____

  _____

- Who are some contemporary heroes of faith who inspire you? Why?

_____

_____

_____

_____

Scripture

Look up the following scripture passages in the Bible translation of your choice. Write them down in the space provided. Discuss how the message can be applied to our world in general and your life in particular. Pray on these passages.

Mark 11:22-24

_____

_____

_____

_____

_____

_____

Psalm 56:3-4

_____

_____

_____

_____

_____

_____

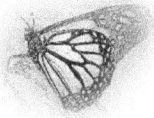

Acts 26:17-18

_____

_____

_____

_____

_____

_____

Proverbs 3:5-6

_____

_____

_____

_____

_____

_____

What can you do to add joy to your life?

_____

_____

_____

_____

_____

_____

_____

Close with prayer. Use your own prayer or the one on page 45 of _Finding Joy in the Morning_.

Notes	My thoughts

4   Live in the Present

Don't clutter your heart and mind with regrets about the past or worry about the future: Live in the moment.

We cannot change the past. We need to accept it, release the guilt and regret, make amends if appropriate, and let it go. We cannot control the future. Worrying about the future creates stress that will make you physically and emotionally ill and does absolutely no good.

Unfortunately, once we have learned the negative habits of regret and worry, it's difficult to unlearn them. But understand that regret and worry are just habits—and like any bad habit, they can be changed and replaced with the positive habit of living in the present.

Trust God to take care of the future while you focus on right now. Take life one day, even one minute at a time. Learn from the past and plan for the future, but live in the present.

Discussion questions (found on page 65 of *Finding Joy in the Morning*, 2nd edition):

- Within the last month, how much time have you spent regretting things that have happened in the past?

_____

_____

_____

_____

_____

- Think of something that worried you to the point that you spent at least five hours thinking about it. What sort of scenarios did you envision in your worries, and how closely did they compare with what really happened?

_____

_____

_____

_____

_____

- Think about someone you've hurt. What should you do to make amends?

_____

_____

_____

_____

_____

- Consider the difference between worrying and planning. Think about a situation you worried about. What happened? Think about a situation you planned for. What happened?

_____

_____

_____

_____

_____

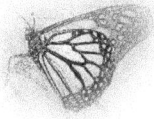

Additional discussion questions:

- Have you ever been in a situation where you were threatened by a natural disaster? What happened? How much notice did you have and how did you deal with it?

_____

_____

_____

_____

- Have you ever hurt or offended someone who refused to accept your apology? How did that make you feel?

_____

_____

_____

_____

- What do you do to relieve stress and worry from your life?

_____

_____

_____

_____

- How does what you think about affect how you feel?

_____

_____

_____

_____

Scripture

Look up the following scripture passages in the Bible translation of your choice. Write them down in the space provided. Discuss how the message can be applied to our world in general and your life in particular. Pray on these passages.

Isaiah 43:18-19

_____

_____

_____

_____

_____

_____

Matthew 6:30-31

_____

_____

_____

_____

_____

_____

Philippians 3:13

_____

_____

_____

_____

_____

_____

Isaiah 41:10

_____

_____

_____

_____

What can you do to add joy to your life?

_____

_____

_____

_____

_____

_____

_____

_____

_____

_____

_____

_____

_____

_____

Close with prayer. Use your own prayer or the one on page 63 of _Finding Joy in the Morning_.

Notes

My thoughts

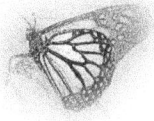

5 Living in Community with God and Others

We are made to live in community—it's one of God's many gifts to us. It is within our relationships with others that we are able to serve and be served.

As much as we need relationships, it's important to recognize that maintaining close relationships with family and friends takes time and effort. It often requires you to take the initiative to do something—from a simple phone call or note to a major effort—to maintain and strengthen your relationships.

The old saying that you can tell a lot about people by the company they keep is true. Your friends are a reflection of you, and you are a reflection of them. The measure of our true wealth is in our friends. How wealthy are you?

That we need God and one another does not mean we are weak. It means we recognize our essential nature, and we are able to find strength in our relationships. It means we know that God works through us, and the only way he can do that is if we are living in community with one another.

Discussion questions (found on page 79 of *Finding Joy in the Morning*, 2nd edition):

- What makes you uncomfortable about needing other people?

_____

_____

_____

_____

- How do you keep in touch with the people you care about?

_____

_____

_____

_____

_____

- Do you find it easy to say "I love you" to the people you love? Why or why not?

_____

_____

_____

_____

_____

- Think of three people with whom you need to reconcile.

_____

_____

_____

_____

_____

- What steps can you take right now to mend those relationships and begin the process of reconciliation?

_____

_____

_____

_____

_____

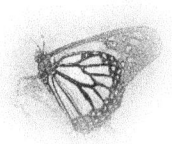

Additional discussion questions:

- Think of your relationship with Jesus—do you feel like you are more of a servant or a friend?

  _____

  _____

  _____

  _____

  _____

- What is one thing you could do within the next two days to strengthen a relationship with a family member or friend?

  _____

  _____

  _____

  _____

  _____

- Consider the others in the group and offer one positive adjective to describe each person.

  _____

  _____

  _____

  _____

  _____

Scripture

Look up the following scripture passages in the Bible translation of your choice. Write them down in the space provided. Discuss how the message can be applied to our world in general and your life in particular. Pray on these passages.

Genesis 2:18

_____

_____

_____

_____

_____

_____

1 Corinthians 7:5

_____

_____

_____

_____

_____

_____

John 15:13

_____

_____

_____

_____

_____

_____

Ephesians 4:2-3

_____

_____

_____

_____

_____

_____

What can you do to add joy to your life?

_____

_____

_____

_____

_____

_____

_____

_____

_____

_____

_____

_____

_____

_____

Close with prayer. Use your own prayer or the one on page 77 of _Finding Joy in the Morning_.

Notes	My thoughts

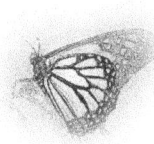

6   Practice Forgiveness

God forgives us. How can we do any less for each other? How can we do any less for ourselves?

Forgiveness is a decision. It's not something you think; it's something you do. It's also a process. It doesn't always happen quickly or easily. And sometimes you have to forgive the same thing over and over.

The act of forgiveness begins with a conscious decision to let go of hurt, resentment, anger, and thoughts of revenge. Those emotions do nothing but drain the joy from your life. They hurt no one but you. When you forgive someone, you are the one who benefits the most because you have eliminated negative feelings from your heart and mind. It's the kindest thing you can do for yourself.

When you forgive, stay focused on forgiving. Don't worry about justice. Don't demand punishment or retribution. Those things won't change what happened. Even though you may think you'll get some satisfaction from watching the person get their just deserts, it won't truly make you feel better—in fact, it may make you feel worse.

Often the person we have the most trouble forgiving is ourselves. When we make a mistake, we must treat ourselves with the same care and compassion with which we treat others. Ask God for forgiveness, then forgive yourself and move on.

Someone else you may need to forgive is God. While God never does anything wrong, we often find him an easy target to blame when bad things happen to us or our loved ones. If you're angry with God, that's okay. He can take it. But you need to forgive him. The process will help you understand what really happened and let God get back to work in your life.

Discussion questions (found on page 89 of _Finding Joy in the Morning,_ 2nd edition):

- Who do you need to forgive?

  _____

  _____

  _____

  _____

  _____

- Have you had the experience of having forgiven someone only to have the negative feelings return? How did you deal with it?

  _____

  _____

  _____

  _____

  _____

Additional discussion questions:

- Do you tend to be quick or slow to forgive? Why?

  _____

  _____

  _____

  _____

  _____

- How has God's forgiveness affected you and your willingness to forgive others?

_____

_____

_____

_____

_____

- What is the best advice you've ever been given about forgiveness?

_____

_____

_____

_____

_____

- If you are sometimes quick and sometimes slow to forgive, what is it about different situations that causes you to respond the way you do?

_____

_____

_____

_____

_____

Scripture

Look up the following scripture passages in the Bible translation of your choice. Write them down in the space provided. Discuss how the message can be applied to our world in general and your life in particular. Pray on these passages.

Colossians 3:13

_____

_____

_____

_____

_____

_____

_____

Luke 17:3-4

_____

_____

_____

_____

_____

_____

_____

Ephesians 4:31-32

_____

_____

_____

_____

_____

_____

_____

Micah 7:18

_____
_____
_____
_____
_____
_____

What can you do to add joy to your life?

_____
_____
_____
_____
_____
_____
_____
_____
_____
_____
_____
_____
_____
_____
_____

Close with prayer. Use your own prayer or the one on page 87 of _Finding Joy in the Morning._

Notes	My thoughts

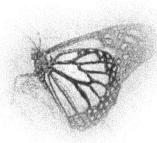

7 Stay Close to God

It would seem like once you ask God to come into your life and you turn your life over to him that staying close to him would be easy. It's not. Evil and worldly temptations will always be there, trying to get between you and God. In some ways, your relationship with God is the one you must work the hardest to maintain.

People who live in a state of consistent peace, no matter what sort of turmoil is swirling around them, do that because they understand the need to stay close to God and they know how to do it. Getting and staying close to God and getting back on his track when you have slipped away takes awareness and effort. It requires daily spiritual exercise of prayer (talking and listening to God), study (learning things that will help you grow in your faith), service (sharing the word of God and helping others in need), and worship (expressing reverence and adoration for God).

When you do your part, God will do the rest.

Discussion questions (found on page 109 of *Finding Joy in the Morning,* 2nd edition):

- What new actions can you take this week to exercise your spiritual muscles?

_____

_____

_____

_____

_____

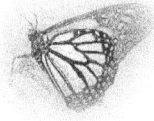

- Which of the spiritual exercises—prayer, study, service, worship—are you most comfortable with? Which one challenges you the most? Why?

_____

_____

_____

_____

_____

_____

- When was the last time you prayed for someone else? Why did you do it, and what happened?

_____

_____

_____

_____

_____

_____

- Can you think of a time when you have felt closer to God than you do now? What was happening then, and how did you move away from him?

_____

_____

_____

_____

_____

_____

Additional discussion questions:

- Have conflicts within your church family kept you from being close to God? How did you handle it? Could you have handled it better?

_____

_____

_____

_____

_____

_____

- How do you usually pray—do you have a set time and place or are you more spontaneous?

_____

_____

_____

_____

_____

- How do you prepare to pray? Do you read scripture or a devotion? Do you just sit quietly? Or something else?

_____

_____

_____

_____

_____

- What occupies most of your time in prayer—adoration, confession, thanksgiving or supplication?

_____

_____

_____

_____

Scripture

Look up the following scripture passages in the Bible translation of your choice. Write them down in the space provided. Discuss how the message can be applied to our world in general and your life in particular. Pray on these passages.

Psalm 145:18

_____

_____

_____

James 4:8

_____

_____

_____

_____

2 Timothy 2:13

_____

_____

_____

_____

Micah 6:8

_____

_____

_____

_____

_____

_____

What can you do to add joy to your life?

_____

_____

_____

_____

_____

_____

_____

_____

_____

_____

_____

_____

_____

_____

Close with prayer. Use your own prayer or the one on page 107 of _Finding Joy in the Morning_.

Notes

My thoughts

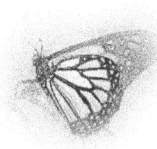

8   The Gift of Problems

Believing in God and being a Christian does not mean that you will live a life free of struggles or hardships. But it does mean that you can face your problems knowing that God is in control and working for and through you to reach a resolution.

Problems can beat us down or build us up. Let your problems build you up. Let them give you strength. Let them teach you something that will make your life better. Remember that God often uses small problems to help prepare us for bigger challenges (and rewards) to come as we serve him.

Don't blame God for your troubles; instead, let him direct you and walk with you so that you can take the action that will get you through the storm. You're always going to get better results if you do things God's way. In fact, the source of our problems is often that we are trying to control things ourselves instead of relying on God. Ask God for help. Let him tell you what he wants you to do. Then do it.

Discussion questions (found on page 119 of *Finding Joy in the Morning*, 2nd edition):

- Think about a problem you have overcome that seemed insurmountable at the time. What did you learn from that experience?

_____

_____

_____

_____

_____

- We often use the term "blessing in disguise" to describe something negative that ultimately turned into a positive. When was the last time you experienced a blessing in disguise, and how did you realize it was a blessing?

_____

_____

_____

_____

_____

Additional discussion questions:

- Has there been a time when someone has helped you see a problem you were experiencing as a gift while you were in the midst of the problem? What did that person do and how could you do the same for someone else?

_____

_____

_____

_____

_____

- Has God ever told you to do something you didn't think was possible? What happened?

_____

_____

_____

_____

_____

- When you are facing a challenge, do you turn to the Bible for answers? Share a time when you have done this, particularly which scripture helped you.

_____

_____

_____

_____

_____

- Can you think of a time when dealing with a problem has prepared you for something bigger and better? How did you feel when you were struggling? When did you realize that the problem you had in the past prepared you for a situation that would come later?

_____

_____

_____

_____

_____

Scripture

Look up the following scripture passages in the Bible translation of your choice. Write them down in the space provided. Discuss how the message can be applied to our world in general and your life in particular. Pray on these passages.

John 16:33

_____

_____

_____

_____

Romans 5:3-5

_____

_____

_____

_____

_____

_____

_____

James 1:2-4

_____

_____

_____

_____

_____

_____

_____

2 Corinthians 4:17

_____

_____

_____

_____

_____

_____

_____

Psalm 46:1

_____

_____

_____

_____

_____

_____

What can you do to add joy to your life?

_____

_____

_____

_____

_____

_____

_____

_____

_____

_____

_____

_____

_____

_____

Close with prayer. Use your own prayer or the one on page 117 of _Finding Joy in the Morning_.

Notes	My thoughts

9   Put God in Control

When God is in control of your life, you will be free to live a life without fear, a life filled with purpose, a life built on a foundation of joy. But God won't take control; he wants you to give it to him. Surrender to God and watch what happens.

Discussion questions

- In what ways does God speak to you?

  _____

  _____

  _____

  _____

  _____

  _____

- How is your life different when you surrender control to God?

  _____

  _____

  _____

  _____

  _____

  _____

  _____

- Are you willing to do what God wants you to do even when you don't understand it? Can you share a time in your own life when you had this experience?

_____

_____

_____

_____

_____

_____

- Do you trust God's timing even when it isn't your timing?

_____

_____

_____

_____

_____

- If you have surrendered control of your life to God, do you find it challenging to stay surrendered? Do you occasionally try to take control of some things? If so, what do you do to turn control back over to God?

_____

_____

_____

_____

_____

- Do you believe that God's plan for you is far better than anything that you might come up with on your own? Can you share a time when you have seen this manifest in your life or in the life of someone close to you?

_____

_____

_____

_____

Scripture

Look up the following scripture passages in the Bible translation of your choice. Write them down in the space provided. Discuss how the message can be applied to our world in general and your life in particular. Pray on these passages.

James 4:7

_____

_____

_____

_____

Jeremiah 10:23

_____

_____

_____

_____

_____

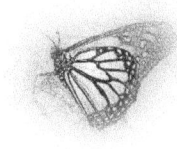

Romans 12:2

_____

_____

_____

_____

_____

_____

2 Timothy 1:7

_____

_____

_____

_____

_____

_____

What can you do to add joy to your life?

_____

_____

_____

_____

_____

_____

_____

Close with prayer. Use your own prayer or the one on page 123 of _Finding Joy in the Morning._

Notes	My thoughts

10   Finding Joy Every Day

We don't have to be going through a crisis to need a little help getting through the day. That help doesn't have to come from miracles or something extraordinary, it can come from doing some purposeful things every day—things designed to bring you joy and create joy for others.

Discussion

Discuss the various things you can do to find joy every day. Share what you have done and what happened.

Scripture

Look up the following scripture passages in the Bible translation of your choice. Write them down in the space provided. Discuss how the message can be applied to our world in general and your life in particular. Pray on these passages.

John 15:11

_____

_____

_____

_____

Ecclesiastes 9:7

_____

_____

_____

1 Peter 1:8-9

_____

_____

_____

_____

_____

_____

Romans 15:13

_____

_____

_____

_____

_____

_____

Nehemiah 8:10

_____

_____

_____

_____

_____

_____

Close with prayer.

Notes

My thoughts

Thank you for being a part of
Intentional Joy.

Join the **Intentional Joy** Facebook group: facebook.com/groups/IntentionalJoy

To learn more about books by Jacquelyn Lynn and to connect with her, visit www.createteachinspire.com.

Like us on Facebook at www.facebook.com/createteachinspire

We'd love to hear from you! If you have any comments about Intentional Joy or would like to share input from your study group, please email FindingJoy@contactTCS.com.

Wishing you grace and peace—and joy
every morning!

TCS

Tuscawilla Creative Services, LLC
P. O. Box 1501
Goldenrod, FL 32733-1501
www.CreateTeachInspire.com
info@contactTCS.com

Finding Joy
in the
Morning
You *can* make it
through the night

Second Edition
Expanded & Updated

Jacquelyn
Lynn

**Let these simple but powerful strategies bring you joy
every morning, even after life's darkest nights.**

Available on Amazon and wherever books are sold.

Finding Joy
J O U R N A L

Jacquelyn Lynn

Use the *Finding Joy Journal* to help you keep track of
what brings you joy, let go of what doesn't and guide you
along your own joyful journey.

Color Your Faith!

Finding Joy in the Morning
Adult Coloring Book

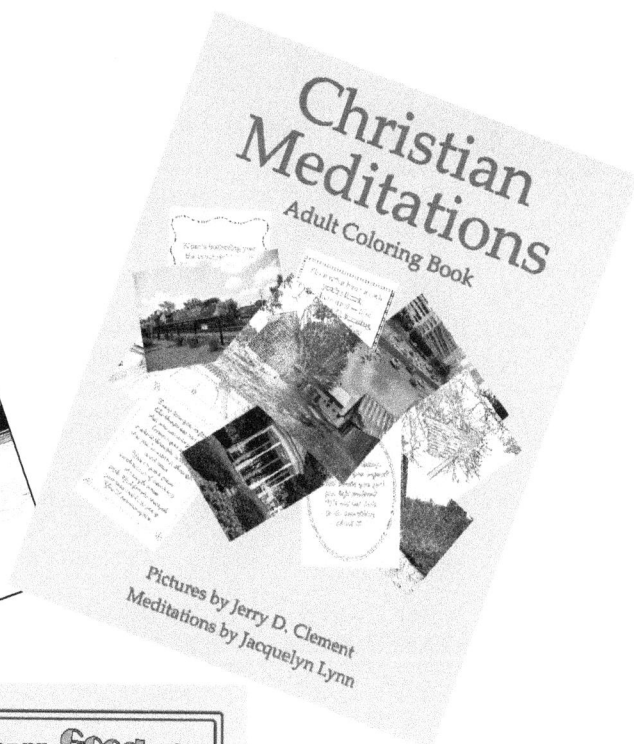

Christian Meditations
Adult Coloring Book

Pictures by Jerry D. Clement
Meditations by Jacquelyn Lynn

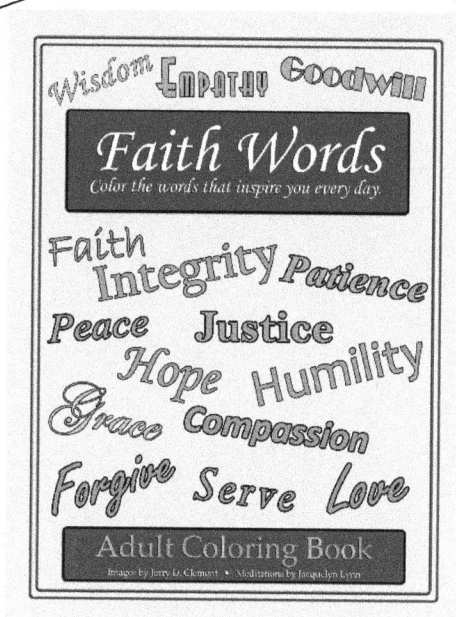

Wisdom Empathy Goodwill

Faith Words
Color the words that inspire you every day.

Faith Integrity Patience
Peace Justice
Hope Humility
Grace Compassion
Forgive Serve Love

Adult Coloring Book
Images by Jerry D. Clement • Meditations by Jacquelyn Lynn

Available on Amazon

Words to Work By

31 devotions for the workplace based on the Book of Proverbs

Jacquelyn Lynn

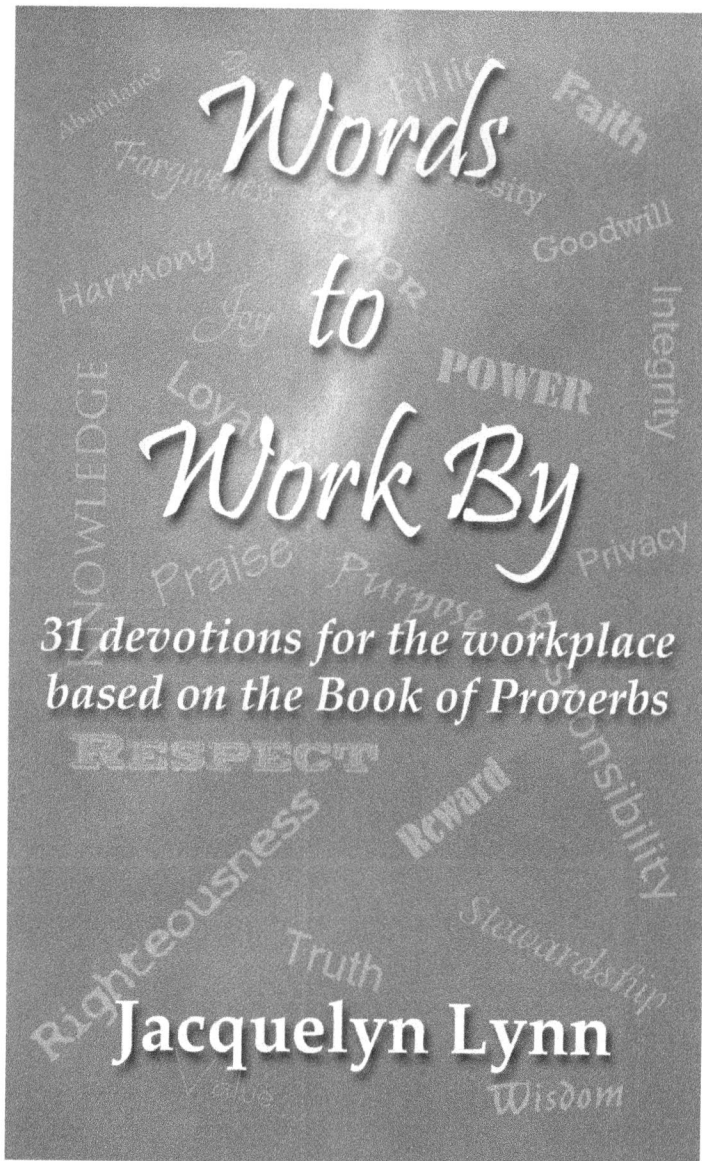

Messages of inspiration and motivation based on the teachings of the world's greatest business advisor: King Solomon. Devotions ideal for beginning your work day, opening a meeting or just taking a break.

Available on Amazon

A Gift to Bring You Joy

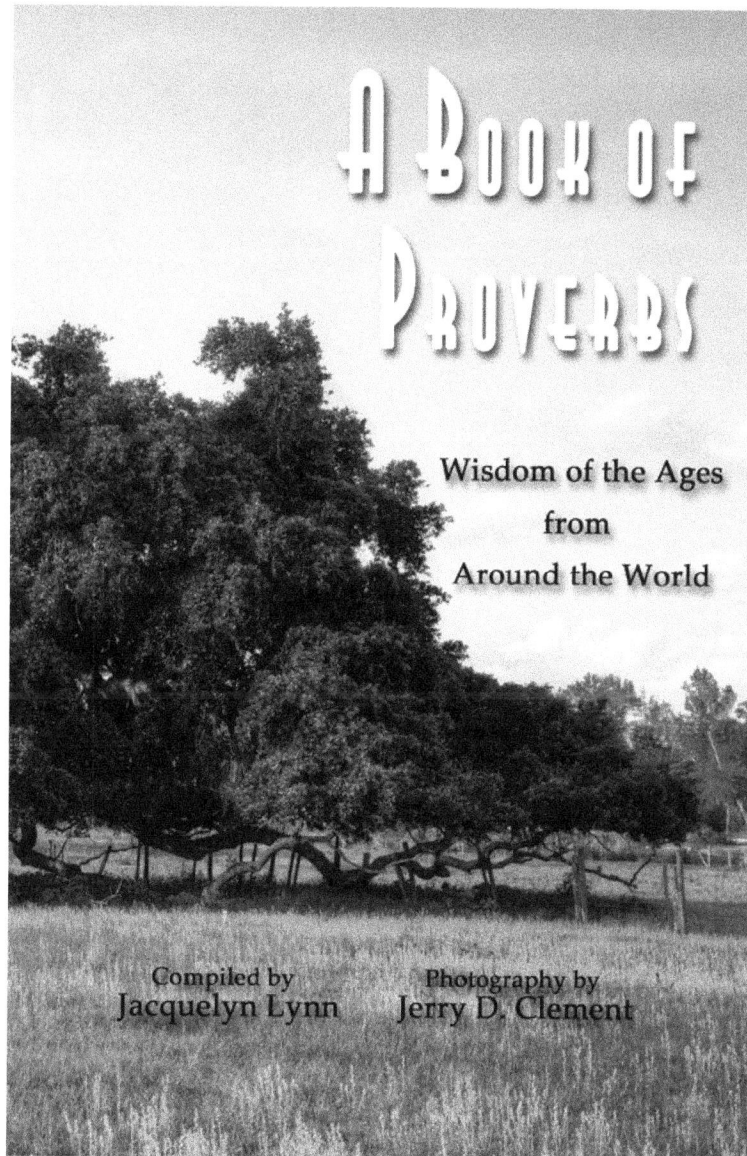

A Book of Proverbs

Wisdom of the Ages
from
Around the World

Compiled by
Jacquelyn Lynn

Photography by
Jerry D. Clement

Download your free copy:

CreateTeachInspire.com/wisdom